HUNTING AND FISHING

GOING UPLAND BIRD HUNTING

BY FELIX PETERS

Gareth Stevens PUBLISHING

Please visit our website, www.garethstevens.com. For a free color catalog of all our high-quality books, call toll free 1-800-542-2595 or fax 1-877-542-2596.

Cataloging-in-Publication Data
Names: Peters, Felix.
Title: Going upland bird hunting / Felix Peters.
Description: Buffalo, NY : Gareth Stevens Publishing, 2027. | Series: Hunting and fishing | Includes glossary and index.
Identifiers: ISBN 9781482482614 (pbk.) | ISBN 9781482482621 (library bound) | ISBN 9781482482638 (ebook)
Subjects: LCSH: Upland game bird shooting--Juvenile literature.
Classification: LCC SK323.P484 2027 | DDC 799.246--dc23

Published in 2027
Gareth Stevens Publishing
2544 Clinton Street
Buffalo, NY 14224

Portions of this work were originally authored by Tom Carpenter and published as *Upland Bird Hunting*. All new material in this edition was authored by Felix Peters.

Designer: Joshua Olson
Editor: Noah Riccardi

Photo credits: Cover, p. 1 Grzegorz Lukacijewski/Shutterstock.com; p. 4 John Scott Leigh III/iStockphoto; p. 6 Jodi Jacobson/iStockphoto; p. 8 Good Focused/Shutterstock.com; pp. 10, 20 Luna Marina/Shutterstock.com; p. 13 kelldallfall/Shutterstock.com; p. 14 temmuzcan/iStockphoto; p. 17 Przemyslaw Wasilewski/Shutterstock.com; p. 18 Cecop Alp/Shutterstock.com; p. 23 Wirestock Creators/Shutterstock.com; p. 24 Igor Zaytsev/Shutterstock.com; p. 27 AirLandSea/iStockphoto; p. 29 Ft. Laud/Shutterstock.com.

Printed in China

Some of the images in this book illustrate individuals who are models. The depictions do not imply actual situations or events.

CPSIA compliance information: Batch #QS27GS: For further information contact Gareth Stevens at 1-800-542-2595.

TABLE OF CONTENTS

CHAPTER 1

WHAT IS UPLAND BIRD HUNTING?

Upland bird hunting is a style of hunting where a hunter walks around a forest or grassy area searching for birds. When they find one, they try to startle the bird so it flies out of hiding. The hunter then tries to shoot the bird. Common upland birds to hunt are grouse, pheasant, and quail.

Black grouse are common upland bird hunting targets.

American Indians were the first people to hunt upland birds in North America. For thousands of years, hunters used snares or traps. Others shot birds using slingshots or bows and arrows.

When European settlers came, they began hunting the birds, too. They also changed the birds' **habitats**. Some of these changes helped the birds. For example, logging and small farms cleared some land. The resulting young forest helped ruffed grouse thrive. Other changes were harmful. On the **prairies**, native grasses were replaced by fields of crops. This hurt populations of prairie chickens.

A man and his dog hunt pheasants in the early 1900s.

In the 1930s, governments started making new laws. These laws helped provide the money needed to protect upland bird habitats. Today, hunters can pursue upland birds in all 50 US states and every Canadian province.

CHAPTER 2

HUNTING ESSENTIALS

In many types of hunting, the hunter waits for **game**. But in upland bird hunting, the hunter walks around and looks for birds. An upland bird hunter may walk many miles in one day. As a result, a pair of sturdy boots is important. Some hunters wear chaps in front of their pants. Chaps protect a hunter's legs from thorns and brush.

Upland bird hunters walk through fields to try to startle birds into flying up into the air.

Upland bird hunters use shotguns. Shotguns fire shells. The shells contain BBs or pellets. The pellets spread out in the air when the gun is fired. This knocks down the birds as they are flying.

Some hunters wear hunting coats. These coats are often made of canvas or other light, tough material. Other hunters prefer to wear hunting vests. Hunting coats and hunting vests both have shell loops for holding shotgun shells.

Hunters try to scare birds out of hiding and cause them to **flush**. Many hunters bring dogs with them. There are different kinds of hunting dogs. Flushing dogs stay

There are many small pellets inside each shotgun shell.

close to their hunters. They help flush birds for hunters to shoot.

Pointing dogs go around or ahead of hunters. When they find birds, they stop and **point**. Then hunters can flush the birds and shoot.

Other dogs find birds that have been shot and bring them back to the hunters.

An English pointer is a popular pointing dog.

These dogs are known as retrieving dogs. Many hunters use whistles to call their dogs to come back.

Hunters may be out all day, so they often bring light foods such as granola bars. They also carry plenty of water.

Hunters should bring water for both themselves and their dogs.

Many hunters also bring **GPS** units. GPS units help them find their way back to their vehicles or camps when hunts are over. Some hunters also carry small knives to clean the birds they have shot.

UPLAND BIRD SPECIES

In North America, hunters can pursue dozens of kinds of upland birds. These include pheasants, quail, grouse, and partridges. Some species are native to North America. Others were introduced from other continents. For example, gray partridges were brought to North America in the 1790s. Ring-necked pheasants were introduced in the 1880s.

CHAPTER 3

FINDING A SPOT

Upland bird hunters choose their hunting spots based on which birds they hope to bag. Some upland birds live in wooded areas. Forests with small trees and lots of brush are good places to find ruffed grouse. Quail and forest grouse often live in woodlands as well.

The most common kind of quail is the bobwhite.

Other types of upland birds live in grassy fields. Ring-necked pheasants live in grain fields and other farmland areas. Prairie grouse can be found in huge areas of short grass. Grasslands are good places to find gray partridges, too.

Some upland bird hunters prefer to hunt alone. Others hunt in groups. Sometimes hunters work together to flush birds. For example, pheasant hunters often work together in two groups. One group lines up and walks through a field. They try to scare up pheasants. The second group of hunters waits at the sides or end of the field. These hunters shoot the birds that fly out.

Hunters need to react quickly to shoot flying birds.

Upland bird hunters change their walking speed often. They may also stop and wait for a while. These techniques make them more likely to startle birds and cause them to flush.

Upland birds fly very fast. If a hunter shoots right at a flying bird, the BBs will miss the bird and go behind it. Instead, the hunter must aim slightly ahead of the bird. This is known as leading the bird. In one leading strategy, the hunter pulls the trigger as the gun's barrel swings past

SKEET SHOOTING

Many hunters use clay pigeons to practice shooting moving targets. Clay pigeons are small discs made of clay. A device called a trap throws the discs into the air. Hunters try to hit the discs before they fall to the ground. This activity is known as trapshooting. Skeet shooting is a kind of trapshooting. In skeet shooting, the trap throws the clay pigeons so that they imitate how birds fly.

Traps help hunters practice their shooting skills before the hunting season.

the bird's beak. Skills and techniques like this that are used to shoot flying birds are known as wing shooting.

CHAPTER 4

STAYING SAFE

Upland bird hunters follow the basic rules of firearms safety. They should always treat guns as if they are loaded. They should keep their fingers away from the triggers unless they are about to shoot. A hunter should also be sure of their target anytime they fire a gun.

Wearing bright colors makes it easy for others to see hunters and their dogs.

Hunters should never point their guns at another person. They should always shoot straight ahead. If they shoot to the side, BBs could hit another person. Many hunters wear eye protection. This can help avoid injuries from any stray BBs.

Upland bird hunters should shoot only birds that are flying. They should never shoot birds on the ground. They could accidentally hit nearby people or dogs.

Hunters should also avoid shooting low-flying birds. It may be tempting to take the shot. But the hunter could accidentally hit a hunting partner or a hunting dog. Instead, hunters should always aim their guns up in the air.

Hunters should shoot higher than where any person could be.

CHAPTER 5

RESPECTING NATURE

Upland bird hunting seasons happen in autumn. This is after female birds have raised their young for the year. During hunting season, hunters should always stay within the bag limit. This is the number of birds a hunter may shoot in one day. Each species of bird has a different bag limit.

The Ruffed Grouse Society helps protect the forests where these grouse live.

The dull-colored female pheasant is called a hen, while the bright-colored male is known as a rooster.

It is best to shoot only male birds. This ensures that female birds will be able to nest again the next spring. However, with most species of upland birds, it can be difficult to tell males and females apart. This is especially true when the birds are flying. Pheasants are an exception. Brightly colored male pheasants are easy to identify. Because of this, it is illegal to shoot female pheasants in all US states and in Canada.

Each hunter must buy a license. Some states require hunters to buy additional stamps, such as pheasant stamps. Money from hunting licenses and stamps helps with **conservation**. It is used to preserve and improve upland bird habitats.

Without good habitats, there would not be any birds to hunt. Many upland bird hunters join conservation organizations. These groups work to make sure the birds have plenty of good habitats. This way, people can continue hunting upland birds for many years to come.

DRIVEN SHOOTING

In the United States, upland bird hunters are always on the move. Hunters and their dogs hike through the wilderness looking for game birds.

In the United Kingdom, things are done a little differently. Teams of hunters wait while people called beaters walk through fields or forests. Beaters try to flush birds and make them fly toward the hunters. This style of hunting is called "driven shooting." Dozens of birds may fly out at once.

Driven shooting became popular in the mid-1800s. For many years, people could hunt only on their own land. But in the 1830s, laws changed. People began inviting hunters to their **estates**. One of these people was Prince Albert. He married Queen Victoria in 1840. And he loved

A painting of a grouse shoot in the mid-1800s.

driven shooting. He invited hunters to shoot at Windsor Castle. Driven shooting became common among the British upper class.

Today, all kinds of people enjoy driven shooting. They often visit historic estates. Places like Drumlanrig Castle in Scotland or Arundel Estate in England are popular destinations.

TEST YOUR KNOWLEDGE

Take this quiz to test your knowledge.

1. Summarize the three strategies to help protect upland bird populations that are described in Chapter 5.

2. What are the advantages of hunting upland birds with a group instead of by yourself? Are there any disadvantages?

3. Which kind of upland bird can be found in the forest?

    A. ring-necked pheasant
    B. gray partridge
    C. ruffed grouse

4. What will happen if a hunter leads too far ahead of a bird when shooting?

    A. The hunter will shoot too late, and the bird will already be gone.
    B. The hunter will miss the bird and shoot the air in front of it.
    C. The hunter will be knocked off balance.

Answers can be found on page 32.

GLOSSARY

conservation
The careful protection of plants, animals, and natural resources so they are not lost, ruined, or wasted.

estates
Places that each have a large house and lots of open land.

flush
To launch into the air and fly away.

game
An animal that is hunted, either for food or for sport.

GPS
A navigation system that uses satellites to figure out location.

habitats
The type of places where plants or animals normally grow or live.

point
When a hunting dog stiffens its body and looks toward a game animal to show the hunter where the animal is.

prairies
Huge, natural grasslands.

FOR MORE INFORMATION

BOOKS

Bailey, Diane. *Bird Hunting*. Minneapolis, MN: Lerner Publications, 2024.

Coulson, Art. *Pheasant Hunting Firsts*. North Mankato, MN: Capstone Publishing, 2022.

WEBSITES

Britannica Kids: Grouse
kids.britannica.com/students/article/grouse/274676
Learn more about grouse, a common type of game bird.

National Geographic Kids: South Dakota
kids.nationalgeographic.com/geography/states/article/south-dakota
Learn more about South Dakota, a popular destination for upland bird hunting.

Publisher's note to educators and parents: Our editors have carefully reviewed these websites to ensure that they are suitable for students. Many websites change frequently, however, and we cannot guarantee that a site's future contents will continue to meet our high standards of quality and educational value. Be advised that students should be closely supervised whenever they access the internet.

INDEX

Answer Key: 1. Answers will vary; 2. Answers will vary; 3. C; 4. B